NEWS FROM

SLIGO

NEWS FROM SLIGO

Amanda L. Irwin

OzarkMountainWritersGuild

Library of Congress Control Number: 2013946551

ISBN – 13: 978-1-940514-01-7
ISBN – 10: 1-940514-01-0

Ozark Mountain Writers Guild
Salem, Missouri 65560

In memory of Bausman, Barney, Canela and Poptart, who taught me to dance in the sun for the first time ever, each day.

In the silence, in
surrounding peace
finally, I hear

June 1

I've decided to occasionally share with you some of my discoveries as we embark upon our journey into country life. I hope you enjoy reading about our adventures.

Roberto called me up the other evening and asked if I wanted five dwarf goats for free. Um, yes. That was all, no word on how to get them here or anything. But maybe we'll have some goats soon. And my chickens, of course. Right now I'm just trying to find the vegetable garden. With all the rain and us not being here, the grass grew about three feet. I tried to mow it with a push mower (I'm glad we don't have neighbors close by, they would have rolled their eyes, as they would have if they had seen me walk my dogs with a leash), and cut about half of it last weekend. I'm developing some enviable biceps. Then I woke up to reality and yesterday I went to Rolla and purchased a riding mower and a trailer to transport it. I guess my introduction to farm life starts with an introduction to suburban yard maintenance. I do learn fast, though. I didn't have any accidents with the trailer (never pulled one before), and I learned how to use the mower while I was riding it (I figured, how would a farmer do it --read the manual? Probably not. So I took a deep breath, downed a cold one and got on out there, just like a farmer would do). I had a blast and I also have a backyard again. Now we'll have to get a tractor. I think I'll read the manual on that, whether a real farmer would or not. A girl could get killed!

Anyway, grass doesn't know that it's not supposed to grow in my garden, so I'll have to weed until I can find the garden, then plant some seedlings.

June 2

I really should get hold of some cut-off overalls before my next ride, and definitely before I get on a tractor. And a big hat. I hope the goats come with instructions; otherwise I'll have to take the riding mower approach (which I guess turned out pretty well). Today was full of discoveries. I awoke to the sound of mooing coming from the neighbors' farm down the road. Nice to know there is life out there besides the surprisingly large black snake I saw while mowing the other day. As I weed-whacked one particularly overgrown corner of the back yard (it is a very large back yard, so you have to imagine this as a particularly large corner), I liberated our little orchard and found wee baby apples, peaches and pears growing. And the blackberry vines that are growing on the fence and everywhere else are flowering --I shall make jam when the time comes (reserve yours now).

I ventured out into the vegetable garden, though it started raining before I was able to get in there with the weed-whacker (thankfully, though, with regular workouts using the heavy duty model I've acquired I won't have to worry about my new biceps disappearing). I was looking for asparagus, which the previous owner's niece told me was in there, somewhere. I found it! But, alas, I am weeks too late. It is not edible now. At least I know where it is for next spring. And, lastly, I discovered an intriguing plant with large leaves and purple flowers; I can't wait to see what that turns out to be.

I plan to approach the barn soon. I've been looking at it a lot lately from this side of the road where the house is. It's really big. And usually pretty muddy.

I know I need to do something with it, but I've got no idea where to begin. I guess going there would be a good start. A few weeks ago I saw a very old, large Great Pyrenees sleeping in there. Haven't seen it since.

News From Sligo

June 12

The City Dog and the Country Dog

The city dog is never very far from his master –the end of the leash or the length of the yard is usually about as far apart as we get. The country dog can sometimes appear as a small speck a half a mile away. The city dog gets her toys at a pet store The country dog makes her own toys, like the walking bone, known by humans as a turtle. The city dog can get a little chunky due to lack of exercise and excess of food. The country dog has a big appetite and runs around a lot on his own secret missions (like turtle hunting). The city dog can sometimes be clean and smell good to a human. The country dog smells good to other dogs, and might occasionally rinse off in the pond. The city dog lives inside and sometimes goes out, while the country dog lives outside and rarely –usually by accident—sets paw inside.

Osito, Bausman and I are learning these differences as they become progressively more countrified. We don't embrace them all. We're having trouble with the inside dog/outside dog thing, which makes the inside of the house not as clean as it could be. And it makes the dogs that were already here when we arrived think Osito and Bausman are weird. Osito just today discovered turtles, and has brought home three, dropping each with a thud at my feet. The first time, when I took it back outside and set it down, he was surprised to discover a few minutes later that his new toy had disappeared, just up and walked away. Kind of magical.

It has been a busy week, moving from Memphis

and Ross still in Florida. It looks as if, with all this space, the golden rule of housekeeping might actually take hold here, eventually: a place for everything and everything in its place. For now, though, I would be happy just to have the boxes gone and their contents anywhere out of sight.

Not too much to report on the farming side of things. While I unpack boxes and put our many belongings away, the grass grows and the apples, pears, peaches and blackberries get a little bigger each day. I believe I discovered a cherry tree out back (assuming that those tiny bright green earring-looking things are wee cherries). Such bliss, I am truly rich. Yesterday I took a few minutes to gather white wildflowers and tiny pink roses for a bouquet. There may be boxes everywhere, but the table is clear and has flowers on it. If I sit just so, and direct my eyes carefully in one direction out to the back yard, I can sit down with a cup of tea and make it all go away.

The pretty plant in the vegetable garden has grown and has more little purple flowers on it. I don't think it's an eggplant.

June 14

The living room window is about six and a half feet high and about nine feet long. It looks out over the front yard, which is probably an acre in size and slopes downhill to the road that long ago went through the middle of the town of Sligo and today separates our house and 65 or so acres from the barn and 25-acre hayfield. Looking out over the shrubs that grow just outside the window, through twenty or so giant oak trees and the lilacs and dogwoods that look like miniatures next to them, I usually see the barn in the middle of the pasture, the line of trees beyond that hide the creek running along the far property line and, on the horizon, the bluish gray silhouette of the Ozark mountains that surround me. Early in the morning the sun rises over those hills and shines golden into our home.

News From Sligo

But this morning is cloudy and cool, light fog covers the road and fields beyond the trees and I see only the outline of the barn roof. The birds chirp, whistle, trill and sing from way up in the treetops to down in the grass, from every direction, near and distant. And a hummingbird, inches from the windowpane, methodically tastes each cluster of tiny white flowers growing on the shrubs that line the outside wall. It was brought here by their dense sweet perfume that also enters through the open windows and fills this room.

I sip my coffee. The dogs sleep. It all runs together through a few grateful gathering tears.

June 18

"Why do they have to kill their new friends? It doesn't seem right." Ross is home. His journey has been long and so much has changed in his absence, including what he understood to be the nature of canines. It's been about three days since I returned the last turtle to its world outside. During most of the time since, Osito has had a few long adventures in undisclosed places and Bausman has enjoyed sitting on the steps sniffing the air, hair flying in the breeze. And then this morning Osito caught his first mole. The four of us had been out in front of the house, amazed at how big our yard is (Ross took a two-hour spin on the riding mower yesterday), how much shade the trees provide, how perfect the view. Ross and I went inside and after a few minutes, I asked him if he knew where Osito was. He looked out, saw him down by the hand pump, and said it looked like he had found another turtle and was playing with it.

Ross hasn't had the privilege of observing that particular relationship, and so he didn't realize that his words could not have been describing the dog with a turtle. So I took a look. Osito would hold very still, nose to the ground, and then suddenly jump back and something small and brown and furry would fly into the air. It didn't take long for Bausman to realize the superiority of this new toy compared to the stuffed dinosaurs, hedgehogs, and other creatures with squeakers that comprise their collection.

I can't imagine that we'll have a mole problem for much longer.

In addition to experiencing moles up close (they

are much softer that I expected, and they look as if they were designed to swim in the dirt with their white paddle feet and their pointy faces), I also learned today that if it looks like it's going to rain, it probably will –even if the weather man didn't say it would.

News From Sligo

24

June 26

Our neighbor Emil has two Great Pyrenees that accompany him when he works in the hayfields. He also sings in a deep bass voice in the harmonic gospel trio, one special song each Sunday in the United Methodist Church of Sligo that is just across our yard. There are usually only twenty or so in the congregation, so you can also identify his voice when everyone sings together.

Today the breeze carries the sounds of his tractor engine and the swishing of the hay turning over, and the smell of diesel mixed with the hay cut yesterday. He finished with his own fields last week and has now started in on ours. Almost every hayfield you can see between here and Salem has been cut, large round bales waiting in symmetric rows like games of checkers among giants.

We have added a new dog with long black hair, a fluffy tail, short legs and a small white spot between his ears. He was hanging out at a drive-in in Ash Flat last week as I was on my way to Memphis. No collar, no owner. He jumped in and off we went. Osito and Bausman are managing his orientation. We're calling him Nico.

News from Sligo

Hayfield, give me a drink

of sun from your

windblown hair

News From Sligo

July 4

The hay is in the barn. We got about fifty bales and Emil got another fifty. I don't expect the horses will go hungry. It's too late to get bees for this year. I'll order them in December so they'll arrive in April or so. I have completely liberated the garden. It was pretty much overrun with hay. I finally finished clearing it all out on Sunday. I have about six terraces, each about 2.5 feet wide and about 30 feet long. I started at the top and have been raking the dried cut weeds to one end, hoeing the leftover growth out, chopping up the dirt with a manual cultivator, and raking the hay back over as mulch. I've made it down to the third terrace. I'm planting a few seedlings I bought at the store, just to have something to show, and I bought some seeds to grow lettuce and a few other greens. I have a little greenhouse and the water supply to the garden runs through it. Viola, the 92-year-old woman from whom we bought the house, informed me that the connection to turn on that spigot is over the ceiling in the laundry room. One day while Ross was away, I decided to get it running. I got up on a chair, moved the ceiling panel over, found the shut-off valve and turned it on. I could hear the water running through and felt proud of myself. Then I went out to the greenhouse and found that the water was spraying out everywhere. The copper pipe that goes from the ceiling of the greenhouse to the garden connection was split all the way down. That repair is going on the bottom of my list. For now, I'm using an outside spigot on the other side of the house and about 150 feet of hose.

Now that the vegetable garden is under control, I can get the chicken house cleaned up, replace the broken windows, cover the other openings with wire mesh and begin preparing for my chickens. Jenny, who lives with her husband Melvin on the farm past Emil's, told me about the small livestock sale every other Tuesday in Salem. I'd like to visit once before I go to buy anything.

Our friend Chris from Chicago volunteered to be our first official house guest, and he arrived on Saturday. We went to Washington, Missouri to pick him up at the train station, which is on the Missouri River. A very nice town with a farmer's market, antique stores, restaurants, bars and wineries all along the river walk. He's my culinary equivalent to a captive audience, and I've been enjoying preparing and planning an array of meals and bakery items. The apples and blackberries are getting ready to pick, so I'm feeling kind of giddy.

News From Sligo

It looks like Osito has figured out that if he sets a turtle down on its back, it won't go away. Yesterday he was enjoying himself in the back yard surrounded by mammoth beef bones he had discovered during one of his adventures and one captive turtle. He looks pretty comical as he proudly trots home with a bone four times as big as his head (I confiscated the turtle and sent it on its way).

July 23

Blackberries are warm to the touch when you pick them. You should only get the juicy, shiny black ones and leave the rest to ripen. How do you know when you have picked enough blackberries? You can never pick enough, but you aren't really having fun anymore when you stop tossing every fourth berry into your mouth. A blackberry vine can trap you by grabbing your sleeve or your hair. It's kind of funny but it can also be painful.

I started seriously getting ready for the horses' homecoming a few days ago –they'll be arriving on Sunday afternoon. I've decided which area they'll be roaming first, so it was necessary to walk around the perimeter and check the fence. I found a few questionable areas and called up Jenny from down the road to ask advice on whom to get to fix the fences. She and Melvin have been getting their fences fixed and said they'd send the man over our way when he was finished; but they also said it would be a while before he'd be finished. She suggested I call Rodney, the fellow who passes the collection plate around at church. He works at the fish hatchery midnight to 8 am and then works on his parents' and his own farm all day every day. I called his mother and she said he was out in a field somewhere but she'd pass on the message. I've had to remind myself that people expect to chat a little before getting down to business. We talked about what a relief the rain was. Rodney agreed to come over this morning at nine to fix the fence. I spent the hour before that cutting away a wild rose vine that would be in his way. I thought to myself that it would make a natural barbed wire fence all by itself.

This has been a good week for seeing new critters. As I was cleaning out the cattle stalls that are now horse stalls, I saw a fuzzy young tarantula. And when Ross and I were driving to Rolla the other day a bobcat ran across the road. Beautiful.

I have more apples than I know what to do with. I think I'll make apple butter and jelly. The peaches are still green. The cherries on the tree I was hoping was a cherry tree are delicious, but they are very small and have surprisingly large pits. I just eat them when I go out there and plan to leave the rest for the birds.

The mysterious purple flowering plant in the vegetable garden is just a plant with pretty purple flowers.

News From Sligo

August 6

Horses walk and sleep on their food. I thought
about this the other morning at about 5:30 when I
looked out the bedroom window and saw Maggie,
Poptart and Canela out in the hayfield, two of them
lying down, the other eating grass and keeping
watch. Imagine getting up in the morning out of a
bed of rice or lettuce. I've been curious about why
they come near when they hear an engine. Maybe
they see us mowing grass and think we are grazing
really fast.

The horses have been here now for eleven days,
and I think I will never tire of looking out across
the back yard and thinking it is the coolest thing in
the universe to see them right there. Or looking out
each window upstairs to see if they are in the
hayfield. I was full of anticipation the weeks

before they arrived. I thought for a long time about where I should put them —on this side of the road or across the road where the barn is. I finally decided it would be better to have them on this side, where they have a smaller hayfield, a pond and about 35 acres of unimproved pasture and woods to explore. And there is a handy three-stall shed just up the hill behind the house. So I cleaned it up, checked the fences, had a few questionable spots repaired and fixed up an old bathtub to use for their water trough. When they got here they seemed to approve of everything. The following day we went to town and when we got back a very large tree had fallen across the fence and on top of the shed, crushing two of the three stalls. I'm very happy that it didn't fall two days before when I was inside of it getting it ready. And that there were no horses in the shed when the tree fell.

There is nothing in the world like the feeling you get when your horse rests her head on your shoulder.

News From Sligo

In your eye the
upside down world
spills out

August 20

Thyme is elusive. You may have already suspected this, and my observations of the herb garden just outside the sun room door confirm it. I planted it along with the basil, oregano, cilantro, and rosemary. They have all thrived, but the thyme has slowly disappeared, kind of slipping through my fingers a little each day. It may have needed more sunlight.

It seems that we are gradually becoming the people I envisioned we would be living here. Aside from a little paperwork, my chores yesterday consisted primarily of moving the horses to the corral at the barn and back, and making bread and peach jam. And my list of upcoming big jobs includes repairing some spots along the fence, fixing some of the gates at the barn, and turning the corral into a round pen. And of course there are the many preparations for the chickens.

Looking back over the past two months, there is observable evidence of progress, mostly attributable to the experience, wisdom and knowledge of our neighbors and fellow church-goers, our visitors, and Mr. Hill, farrier, horse-whisperer, cowboy, fireman, all around American hero and reference for anything regarding country life, who has patiently responded to my requests for help and advice and who has rarely, if ever, laughed at my ignorance.

The hay grew relentlessly and Emil cut, baled and stored it, and now there is more than enough for the horses and anyone who wants to buy some. The garden was an impenetrable jungle, and now there are watermelons, peppers, butternut and acorn and zucchini and summer squash, pumpkins, cucumbers and more tomatoes that one can imagine. In July there were too many blackberries to pick, and now I have several jars of jam. The first two weeks of August brought nearly a hundred sweet white peaches, and there are apples everywhere. And there will be ripe pears soon. In the middle of January I'll be able to open a jar of jam and some summer will spill out. And the horses are here, apparently safe in their pastures and continuing with their training.

Of course there is so much to be done, but I know there always will be. It seems the trick is finding a way to go along with the flow of time. All the weeds and vines and brambles and even the ticks and chiggers and poison ivy will eventually disappear along with the vegetables and fruit that suddenly ripen and demand that I do something with them. I know I'll wake up one morning in November and wonder what happened, how it all could have passed so quickly. And a few months later, one by one, they'll all return. Time is elusive, but if you wait, it will come to you.

September 14

We seem to be having a little trouble keeping our trees vertical. It began in July when the 100+ year-old oak tree fell on the horse shed the day after the horses arrived. During a recent thunderstorm, one of the apple trees fell over. Another of the trees had already fallen quite some time ago and was growing horizontally but still producing healthy apples. For this reason, this season's applesauce, apple butter and jelly shall be named with the prefix "Sideways".

So I called Mr. Don, who runs a tree service. When he answered my call, I said I had an apple tree that had fallen over and I would like to know if he could come out and put it back. He chuckled and said, "We don't put trees back, we remove them". So I asked if he knew of someone who could do the job. He suggested that I consider removing the tree, since after its roots had been exposed for a few days there was little chance it would survive even if it were returned to its original state. I then said I would like to begin the conversation over, and told him I had an apple tree that had fallen and would like to have it removed.

I enjoyed his visit very much, and I suspect he had a pretty good time as well. Don Sr. is at least in his seventies and he does the estimates, while Don Jr. does the "real work". He brought his three Labradors with him in the truck, and we spent about an hour touring the trees around the house and in the orchard. He filled me in on his time in the Navy, the infamous fire on his aircraft carrier during the Vietnam war, life philosophies of Ozark folks, and, of course, tree basics. Now I can look at a cross section of a trunk and count the years it lived and which of those years were dry or had abundant rainfall. I also know why it is important to remove dead limbs and prune regularly in the fall, when the sap is down, not in the spring. Two apple trees and a pear tree will be removed later this fall, after I've harvested the fruit and the leaves are off. Then we'll have a considerable supply of firewood and mulch.

One of the many lessons I have learned from the several chapters of The Tree Ordeal of 2008 is that much is to be gained through being quiet and waiting. When the oak tree fell, I assumed no one but Ross and I had noticed it, and I was a little anxious about what we would have to do. However, two or three weeks later, Bob, on whose property the tree had lived, spent three days chopping and hauling until nothing was left but what was on our shed. And then Emil's son, Emil

Jr., a.k.a. E.J., offered to remove the rest and repair the shed for a jaw-droppingly affordable fee.

I felt a similar anxiety when the apple tree fell, but during the time I spent with Mr. Don, the more I kept my mouth shut the more I learned. Now I will gather my apples --it will be so much easier now to reach the ones on the top--, enjoy the whole apples in the autumn thing, and wait until mid-October when the time will be right to let the trees go. And then we shall enjoy their aroma as they warm us through the next couple of winters. And their mulch will protect and feed the next generation of apple and pear seedlings that Don Sr. taught me how to grow.

Imagine everything that is in a little jar of apple butter.

News from Sligo

*Thanks, tree, for
the sweet red planet
from your universe.*

News From Sligo

October 13

A mother hen must consider her responsibility very seriously. The way her beak frowns when her mouth is shut, and her dark round eyes that rarely blink, give her an air of stern dignity and express that she knows what she is doing. And her obsessive focus on her chicks –any chick she hatches from any egg placed under her, whether she laid it or not, even if it isn't a chicken, she will consider her own-- reveals that she lives exclusively to ensure their health and survival. The chicks are little magnets under and around her, obeying her movements and sounds, then quieting down and getting fluffy quiet to her low clucking as she gathers them under her wings.

At church on Sunday last week I told Melvin and Jenny that I had everything prepared as they had suggested –an old doghouse with a new secure door facing a rabbit hutch where the chicks can be outside and pick at the grass during the day. Later that afternoon I went over to get them: nine peeping days-old chicks, two white and the rest red, and their no-nonsense red Ameraraucana brood hen mother. I named her Helen.

There is really no point in trying to describe the range of colors from blood red to bright gold and orange to dull brown as the trees and bushes are transformed every day under the autumn sun. A pamphlet from the nature center in town explains that with fewer hours of sun and cooler nights, the chlorophyll is breaking down in the leaves and the yellow carotenoids that have been there all along are now visible, along with red and purple that result from sugar produced during the warmer days that is trapped in the leaves during the cool nights.

It's somewhat humbling to be reminded that this is happening for reasons other that to inspire humans to consider the mysteries behind a natural world that is not only a community of millions of organisms thriving and dying in a perfect chain of symbiotic interdependence, but that also is beautiful beyond reason.

I am comforted as I watch and consider how, as the lush green world I have been observing every morning at sunrise begins to die, it pours out its life with such astounding generosity, flaming showers of color.

On the second evening of our new family of chicks, we arrived back from town shortly after the sun had set. The hutch was knocked askew in front of the doghouse door. The nine chicks huddled silently together in one dark corner. The only trace

News From Sligo

of Helen, a few of her soft perfect red feathers.

News from Sligo

Alone, a star

waits while

the sky comes around

News From Sligo

November 13

The cold weather and the recent change back to standard time have resulted in changes to our daily routine. When we get up it is completely dark outside, and if it is a clear morning there is a blanket of stars. The dogs and I go out back to gather twigs and small branches to get the fire going in the fireplace. Then they eat their kibble –a very affordable recent discovery-- and I make my coffee, and we sit in front of the fire in sleepy stillness, watching the flames, meditating and planning our day. Among recent activities has been picking up the last pears that have fallen and making pear butter; the last batch will be finished today. When the sun comes up I go out to the chicken house and open their little trap door so they can walk up their plank and out into their grassy run. I get their feed out of an old freezer recycled as a rodent-proof storage bin, and check their water.

I don't know, but I would estimate that our chickens might live under the tightest security of any chicken around. After spending about six weeks in the canning room, they recently moved into the chicken house. Many of those days were dedicated to acquiring a few hundred square feet of wire mesh, digging around piles of old lumber to find usable boards, lining one 50' side of the building with wire mesh, replacing four entire windows and about fifteen window panes, borrowing Mr. Hill's circular saw and having John up to design, direct and carry out the framing of the approximately one hundred square foot chicken coop, and the lining of the walls and ceiling with wire mesh. I don't think even a mouse could get in. The entire building, with a large run on one side, is surrounded by an electric mesh fence installed with the help of Stephen, Chris, and Stacey, who came up from college in Memphis during fall break. And above much of the open space outside is a poultry netting cover to protect against birds of prey. Helen's orphans are about 3/4 of their adult size and enjoy hopping in and out of their trap door, eating grass and bugs, dusting themselves, and roosting. When they sunbathe, they lie down sideways and unfold one wing so the sun's heat reaches the downy part underneath. They look uncharacteristically awkward and lopsided when they do that. The rest of the time they seem surprisingly agile and self-sufficient, considering their state of armlessness.

The church service a couple of weeks ago would have seemed a little horrifying to me in previous times. During the part when the pastor asks for special concerns, we discovered that the day before, Allen had been operating a tractor or dozer when something malfunctioned, and while repairing it he almost completely severed his index finger. And Jenny reported that after a hayride, her niece lifted her eighteen-month-old child from the trailer and set her down, to be rolled over moments later and fatally crushed when the tractor pulled away. I have learned that people here live and die intensely, for the most part.

This past Sunday, after we sang the first hymn, Jeannette the pastor asked any vets present to step to the front. I repressed a laugh at myself when I realized that she was referring not to veterinarians, but veterans. From the fifteen or so people present, two men who served their country during WWII and three who served during the Vietnam war quietly walked to the front and stood, the same inscrutable expression on each of their faces. Jeannette said they had gone places the rest of us never had to go, and seen and done things the rest of us never had to. And, following her example, we hugged, thanked, and congratulated each one of those men. And we sang America the Beautiful and My Country 'Tis of Thee, and for the first time in a very, very long time, I was genuinely moved by the meaning of the words we sang and I was humbled by the smallest notion of what thousands upon thousands of men like my neighbors have sacrificed.

In four days deer season starts and it will continue for ten days. Around here, hunting is as profound a tradition as the celebration of our nation's Independence, and almost as much a symbol of freedom as the stars and stripes. Last Thursday, some of the women at the Arts & Crafts Guild meeting and I were imagining the potential benefits of outfitting our horses and dogs with special reflective vests made of hunter orange fabric. They told me of seasons past when they would see folks driving back home with "game" such as goats and calves tied to the front grills of their trucks. It is a puzzling mix of excitement, respect and ridicule. I just plan on keeping my horses and dogs close by, and will assume that no hunter, however blind, neglectful or ignorant, could mistake a chicken for a deer.

November 30

The day Barbara brought her first-born baby home from the hospital, she carried him across the creek to the house because the water was too high for the truck. Her husband Lewis offered to take her arm and guide her, but she was used to crossing the creek by herself and was afraid leaning on him might throw her off balance, and then she might drop the baby. Steven is now about thirty-eight and suggests that this early stream crossing might explain why he loves to go whitewater kayaking and canoing. I had the pleasure of meeting him a couple of days ago because he is home from Oregon for Thanksgiving. Barbara called in the morning to see if we would like to come over and meet him since he has so much in common with Ross. When she found out that Ross was in Colorado, she still let me come. I made a pie in hopes that she wouldn't regret it.

Their farm is only a mile or two away from us as the crow flies. However, not being a crow and not in the mood for an hour's hike over and another back, I decided to drive five miles over surprisingly rugged terrain. I got lost; I was glad to have 4-wheel drive; I thought I had finally arrived at their house when Kathy greeted me at her door and explained where I had gone wrong —a road a few miles away, that I had thought ended at a gravel pit, in reality continued on as a gravel road to the farm's gate. Both farms are in the middle of the Indian Trail Conservation Area, which consists of 13,503 acres of woods, hills and rocks. Barbara and Lewis raise Hereford bulls in a large valley of pasture below rolling hills. One can cross the creek nowadays over a concrete low-water bridge that is still always a few inches under water.

The house, yard, barn, out-building, pastures, one truck and one tractor are neat and clean. Nothing is out of place. Lewis is seventy years old and looks about fifty. He cuts and bales his hay with only a little hired help, and he chops enough wood to keep their furnace running every day all winter long. When Barbara showed me their enclosed front porch, I saw a line of wood about thirty feet long and four feet high. I asked how long that would last. Three days or so.

Their house was a 15' by 15' two-room (one up and one down) log home a hundred years ago. They have added on to make it about three times that size, but even so, I have never been in a more austere space. They have everything they need, and nothing more. They have two wardrobes where they keep all their clothes, and one closet with a few linens. A small television sits unnoticed in a corner of the living room; it receives three stations through a very tall antenna outside. The most recent innovation in their telecommunication is the push-button phone with which the telephone company replaced the dial phone, at no charge, several years ago.

During my two-hour stay I learned of their life over the past forty years or so, raising Steven and Elaine, and farming. Our conversation was rich, and those years and days came alive for me. Steven told me about his time in graduate school, his work as an environmental consultant and his new job at a university in Oregon; and he showed me breath-taking pictures of the mountains and rivers in eastern Oregon. We ate pie and laughed. Barbara showed me the upstairs, the attic that has always been a living space. Wallpaper from at least as far back as the 1950s lined the slanted ceiling and walls in two small rooms, and dozens of school awards from Steven and Elaine's childhood through high school covered the space on the walls. Near a far window a small bookcase holds a collection of toy horses, the Lone Ranger and Tonto from almost sixty years ago when Barbara was a child. This room was the only place in the entire 500 or so acres, it seemed, that was filled with objects. It was not easy tearing myself away to go home. I felt so comfortable there, a place so empty of things and so full of human life.

Recently I heard someone say that often-repeated phrase about marriage being nothing more than a piece of paper. It seems like something I might have believed at one time, but I look around me and see that it is not so. Gilbert and Joanne came to church today with their son Danny, a large, sixty-something tattooed biker, his daughter and son-in-law, and his very plain, gray-haired, slightly overweight fiancée, whom he introduced by saying that his prayers had been answered because she would marry him in February. His voice was shaky as he introduced his daughter as the most precious thing in his life. I looked over at her and tears were streaming down her cheek. At that moment, watching those six people between thirty and eighty years old so tearfully rejoice in this engagement, it crossed my mind that only some previous loss and longing for the completeness that is love could cause such profound contentment at having gained it in the present.

I don't know if the people around here are happier in their marriages than in other places where I have been, but it seems so. It could be that they they've worked together and sacrificed together to keep their families going, and so have grown closer. It could be that there is more time and less clutter here, so they can more easily see what they have and think about what it is worth and learn to cherish it more. Or that they just expect less and so are not disappointed. They don't seem to need to invest excessively in making themselves appear more attractive to each other; their love and affection don't seem altered one way or another by beauty, slenderness, well-defined muscles and such. The attraction and affection originate somewhere else, and seem to run deeper than I've imagined.

Marriage might be just a piece of paper, as is a building permit for a house. With the permit a builder can put up another house or a person can build a home. The difference is in the amount of one's self mixed in with the careful intention that goes into cutting each board, driving each nail; the thought invested in planning where each wall will go, where each brick will be placed; then, each piece of furniture. And in how one takes pains to maintain and repair the home and make it cozy, to keep it safe and warm because it is one's source of comfort and strength, the embodiment of one's hopes. Sometimes one breaks one's back with the heavy stuff, or hammers a finger driving a nail. People strain themselves and get injured or resentful, but they do what they must to hold their home together. Sometimes all one can do is keep it from falling in on itself or going up in flames. Every ounce of energy, every word, gesture, tear and silence becomes like the brick or like the mortar, it is who we are and provides our place in the world.

I suspect that what brings Steven all the way

across the country once a year at Thanksgiving to the modest home where he grew up, might somehow be the same as what brings tears streaming down the cheeks of that huge, aging Harley man as he slips his arm around the waist of his fiancée.

News From Sligo

December 17

There is a thick layer of clouds covering the valley that is Sligo. The ground is hard, frozen. The air cuts at the skin. The world outside seems to sleep in almost complete silence. If you stand still for a few minutes, however, you hear the chickadees chirp; squirrels rustle in the leaves; chickens scratch in the long grass that hides them. The horses make an almost imperceptible swish as they pull mouthfuls of hay off the bale, frosty backs and tails.

It seems appropriate to take stock and consider some of the lessons from this year. The surprisingly numerous aspects of our relationship with time comprise the most striking discovery. One invests perhaps too much in efforts to save time; it is simply there, allowing us to live the hours and days that become our lives. The work here is not hard; rather, it requires strength and time. And one improves with experience. There sometimes appear to be an overwhelming number of jobs that need to be done immediately. It helps to make a list, cultivate patience, and begin with what's in front of you. The satisfaction that results from accomplishing these jobs more than compensates the effort. So much can be gained from acting at the right moment. There is no point in hoarding anything, although it is necessary to plan for later, put away enough to get through the winter. Then, indulge in the pleasure of sharing the surplus. The sound of complaining makes it very difficult to hear opportunity knocking. The best cure for wanting more is accepting the challenge of understanding how rich we are. Love really does know no bounds. Keep your eyes open –if not, you are sure to miss the treasures set before you. We exist within a community, independent of our desire to.

The moon in recent days has appeared unusually large. When the sky is clear it shines on the horses in the pasture, the barn roof, the trees and hills in the distance, bringing everything a little more into focus. Maybe it's being away from cities and towns, secluded in this quiet valley; maybe it's just the time of year. But it is easy right now to believe that somewhere out there an angel is watching over us.

News From Sligo

January 29

Things I have learned this winter. You can never have too much firewood, but it is plentiful and free, and splitting logs is a good way to get warm on a cold day; plus it gives you the illusion of being really strong. However, you must have a chainsaw for cutting the logs and a maul for splitting them; you cannot get by with a hand saw and whole logs will not burn for long, if at all. One should not be seduced by the idea that before chainsaws people did it all by hand. In the olden days people must have planned ahead better and been stronger and more persistent than we are. You can probably save money by not buying electric heaters for the horses' watering trough and the chickens' waterer, but you will spend a lot of time pounding holes in 4-inch thick layers of ice and carrying buckets, waterers and garden hoses around. When you finally get a frozen garden hose to thaw enough for the water to push out all the ice inside, it looks like the little cylindrical ice pellets from soda fountains and hotel ice machines. It is easier to hike in the woods during the winter, and there are no bugs or poison ivy. Just because it's freezing cold outside most days doesn't mean you should stop applying flea and tick control to the dogs and horses. The more time you spend outside, the more hot chocolate you can drink in front of the fire. Naming an animal is not something you should do without considering carefully whether it is wise to do so in the first place. There are an infinite number of varieties of seeds to plant in the spring, but there is a finite amount of space in the garden and energy available for tilling and weeding. This is the perfect time to locate the blackberry vines to visit in July. There are many good reasons to keep bees and few reasons not to.

You should always assume there will be a power outage and you must do all you can to prepare for it. In fact, in just about everything, prepare for the worst and hope for the best.

Almost four weeks ago on a Saturday morning, a horse and a mule came walking along the road and up our driveway, into the backyard. I thought it might be a good idea to get a halter on one of them and guide them into a pasture so they would be safe until their owner found them. They were a little spooked, and every time I got within a few feet of them, they would trot away. After twenty minutes or so, we were at least a half-mile down a side road and I needed to go meet my goat milk lady who was only going to be at our meeting place for 30 minutes, so I left the horses and wished them well. When I got back home with my milk, they were in the front pasture. I've since asked all the neighbors and none of them helped them through the gate. All of our friends and neighbors spread the word to everyone they knew who owned horses; we called the sheriff's office and the veterinarian and put an ad on the board at the MFA. After three weeks, I named the paint gelding Manchas and the little grey mule Rucio, and let them into the pasture with my horses (by this time, the mares were very expressive about their wishes to have them over). I spent almost an entire day watching them get to know each other, going from screeches and kicks and pinned ears to sniffing noses and rubbing necks. They would tear down the hill and across the field at top speed, all in a line, then stand around deciding who could be in the group and who had to be put out for awhile. Eventually each one found its place and they merged into a herd.

The women at the Sligo Community Arts & Crafts Guild remarked that people are starting to abandon their horses in the nearby national forest, now that the economic crisis is deepening. The Arts & Crafts Guild meets every first and third Thursday. We all bring lunch and share knowledge on crocheting, knitting, embroidery, chair caning, and a variety of other talents and abilities traditional to life in the country. Needless to say, I have no knowledge of this type to share, but someone has to be there to learn what the others are teaching, so my role is important. I consider Marie to be my own personal crochet and embroidery tutor. She is small and seems fragile, a sweetness in her smile like she's always known me, loving blue liquid eyes and neat white hair. Her fingers are crooked with arthritis and she always has a hug for me. She explains so clearly, she makes me believe I can do anything at all. I have a square to embroider that will be part of the next quilt. The one that is almost ready to be assembled now is missing only two squares, one of them from Viola, the woman who, together with her husband, designed our house and lived in it for thirty-some years. I'm sure they'll be ready by the next meeting. All of the other squares were laid out on a long table. The design was a fan, a ribbon, two doves and a few flowers. Each woman had chosen her own thread colors and embroidered her name under the design. They will all be sewn together, each one held in place by two, three or four of her companions, forever into the quilt. As in a photograph, they have joined hands and captured a moment in time.

We all share our food and sometimes our recipes. The soups have been so delicious that it looks like we will soon organize a soup cook-off to raise money for the community center roof.

It won't be long before the chickens produce their first eggs, so I need to either purchase a nest or improvise one good enough to convince the hens that it is the ideal spot to lay an egg. Hens like to do this in privacy, so I'll put it in the darkest corner of the chicken house. Each hen lays an average of one egg per day. I have two hens and five roosters. If you leave the eggs in the nest instead of gathering them every day, eventually there will be a clutch and a hen will go broody and sit on them until they hatch, assuming they are fertilized. With five roosters, I don't think that will be a problem. Perhaps in this way I can improve the hen-to-rooster ratio. That and some chicken & dumplings.

Last Wednesday a woman named Pat left a message on our phone. She said she heard that her son's paint horse and small gray mule were at our place and asked that we call back. I later spoke with Jenny, and she told me that Pat's family used to run the sale barn in town. Jenny had asked the auctioneer to announce the found horses, and her husband was there. So one of these days Manchas and Rucio will go back to being whoever they were before, and Maggie and Canela and Poptart will be a herd of three again. But until they go, I will brush their faces and scratch their ears and clean the goo out of Rucio's eyes every day.

February 18

I suspect one indication that winter is coming to an end and spring is imminent is the appearance of skunks. I've been helping out Jenny at her diner at the sale barn for the past couple of weeks, and when we aren't busy we talk about the various animals, people and events in our lives. She mentioned this week that the smell of skunk was very apparent around their house.

We've been having a little trouble lately with one of the dogs, Osito, who likes to stay outside when we are ready to go to bed. So last night was the second time we decided to leave him out and let him in sometime during the night when one of us might wake up. I got up at two and there he was at the door, eager to come in. And in his wake the overwhelming evidence of an encounter with a skunk. I'm considering it one more phase in a sort of hazing experience for the city dog. As soon as I got back into bed I realized there was no way his situation could wait until morning. He was already rolling around on rugs and dog beds, so off we went to the downstairs shower. I gathered dog shampoo and a can of tomato sauce (I've heard tomato juice is good and we didn't have any) on the way. My seven step improvised method seems to have worked: wash with dog shampoo, massage with tomato sauce for five minutes and rinse, wash with bath soap and rinse, wash with shampoo and rinse, massage with conditioner for five minutes and rinse; blow dry and spray generously with dog grooming deodorizing and conditioning spray. He smells fine now, but the rest of the night our dreams were saturated with that special aroma he left behind in every spot he touched before the bath.

And just in case we missed the message, Ross and recently adopted Pele encountered yet another skunk during an excursion this morning. Fortunately, both of them had the good sense to keep their distance.

News From Sligo

Leaves or birds burst out
flying to the ground
falling to the air

March 7

The fields are beginning to turn green, short thin blades emerging. Bluebirds fly over the road and sit on the barbed wire fences. Skunks and opossums are everywhere. The spring peepers have been peeping for a few weeks now. They are tiny tree frogs, and there is no way to describe their music. A couple of days ago I witnessed for the first time a calf being born. I went to Melvin and Jenny's to get the keys to the Community Center and as I waited at the back door, I noticed that up on the hill, one of the cows had a large bubble under her tail. I told Melvin and he said she was having a calf and that was the water. So we sat inside at the kitchen window and watched and cheered and laughed and moaned as she lay down and pushed and the baby made its way out and she licked it as it tried to stand up, and it fell over. It got its rear feet under itself and got halfway up and fell onto its face. It got its front feet up and fell on its behind. After an eternity, it stood up. Then it began looking for the milk. Under her chest, and she moved its head back. It found the udder and another eternity passed while it struggled to figure out how to use it. Up the hill a little, another calf that was born the night before ran and jumped along behind its mother. It's calving season. I am in awe.

That evening, the Sligo United Methodist Church Ladies catered the Cattlemen's dinner at the Commons, the fairgrounds in Salem. I needed the key to the Community Center because Jenny and Vivian had forgotten the salad bowl when they were there earlier in the day. I arrived at the Commons kitchen at about four o'clock that afternoon and Marie, Jenny, Vivian, and Sarah were all there, cooking, preparing, chatting, laughing. Over the next two hours, four more Sligo Ladies arrived and joined in the work. I told them about the calf, and they began asking each other how many calves they thought they might have seen born in their lives. Marie looked upward, put a finger to the side of her chin, "too many to count." But they shared the excitement with me and described the last few days, looking for cows about to have their calves, walking and riding four-wheelers all over their hundreds of acres, searching the creeks and woods, and counting the two or three or four that had been born in a day.

Since we joined the church and I have become a Sligo United Methodist Church lady, we have catered the Friday Night Dance at the City Hall in Salem and the Cattlemen's dinner. Today Danny is getting married at our church, and the ladies decorated the church and are catering the reception.

And then, the big day: Sligo Fest is next weekend. There will be corned beef and cabbage, reuben sandwiches, Irish stew, and all kinds of fun, music and activities for all ages. It seems this group of women is pretty well known for the quality of the food they prepare and serve. Being one of them is like living in a firm and soft embrace.

The world changes in the spring. Winter was relatively quiet; not much happened. But suddenly in came Osito smelling like a skunk, and a few days later he gave me my first lesson in how opossums play opossum. He brought it to the back door and dropped it at my feet. I was surprised at the size and shape of its teeth, as it lay there dead. With the tip of my boot, I turned it over to see the other side, to check how heavy it was. I finally picked it up by its tail to keep the dogs from eating it, and I placed it in the wheelbarrow. Twenty minutes later it had disappeared. It might be the same opossum I found in the chicken's electric fence a few days ago, halfway in and suffering a little seizure every two seconds when the electric current went through. I pulled it out by its tail and tossed it a few feet away.

I've received my vegetable seeds and cleaned out the greenhouse. I am gradually clearing the garden and have opened it up to the chickens, who are helping me till. The time came when it was clear that I could not postpone dealing with the hen-to-rooster ratio any longer. The roosters were ganging up on each other and abusing the hens and things were getting out of hand. Two weeks ago I killed my first chicken and was surprised to discover that the word "pluck" is onomatopoeia. The hens are grateful and have rewarded me with eggs this week. I was so excited about the first egg that I blew out the white and yolk, ate a scrambled egg and saved the shell, kind of like casting Baby's first shoes in copper. I also had the best chicken vegetable soup I have ever tasted.

Emil suggested we advertise the sixty or so bales of hay in our barn for $20 each. We will be selling the last bales this weekend if all goes as planned. As I look out every morning and see the hayfield slowly turning green, I remember watching him cut and bale that hay last summer. Our history will soon complete one cycle.

Here is a recipe for a simple country cake. You can frost it, cover it with fruit, or eat it plain:

3 cups of flour

1 3/4 cup sugar

2 1/2 tsp. baking powder

dash of salt

1 1/4 cups milk

1/2 cup oil

2 eggs

Mix dry ingredients and wet ingredients (you can add 1 tsp. vanilla if you want) separately, then combine and mix on low until it's mixed and on high for 4 1/2 minutes. Pour into greased and floured 13 x 9 inch or two 8 or 9 inch diameter pans, and bake at 350 for about 40 minutes.

News From Sligo

The sky sinks its gray
fingers into the earth and
pulls out sunny daffodils

April 24

It all started with the furry buds on the giant pussy willow outside the dining room window. The days were still pretty much wintry short and gray; snow fell now and then. But as the winds picked up and March arrived, there were definite signs: a pair of bluebirds shopping around for a new house, the eerie whine of the spring peepers in the evening. The pear trees blossomed white and the bees were an engine humming overhead; then the peach tree in the corner of the orchard; and when the apple trees finally filled their branches with pink flowers, the temperature dropped below freezing and I borrowed a tarp from Melvin and gathered some old sheets from the garage and tried to cover them, afraid the promise of this summer's fruits would vanish.

It turned out it was only below 32 for a few hours

and the trees are fine. Eventually green leaves began to appear as the jonquils and finally the tulips came out; and now the lilacs sweeten the warm air and the dogwood is lacy white, and both release an occasional petal, fluttering butterflies.

The hens must be relieved as they each give me one pastel greenish turquoise Easter egg daily. They share one rooster. I couldn't bring myself to kill any more chickens this spring, so I pinned a slip of paper on the bulletin board at the MFA: one beautiful Araucana rooster, free. The next day a man called, then came to pick him up, asking if we had any more animals we didn't want, and the following Tuesday at the small livestock auction, I recognized that man and noticed familiar greenish-black tail feathers protruding from a cage filled with chickens, and I admired his resourcefulness.

One recent Monday, as I returned to the diner from delivering coffee to bidders around the auction ring, I saw a tall, thin elderly woman in the kitchen talking to Jenny. I hadn't seen Viola (who turned ninety-three this March) for over a year, and she always seems to me more like a loving ghost that lives with us at the house, along with John, who really did pass away a few years ago, and watches over us from his spot in the cemetery up the hill. I have developed what I believe to be a kind of intimate understanding of Viola, along with a unique love, as I have discovered traces of her in the constant show of flowers from March through September, in the asparagus and garlic and the mysterious plants with the pretty little purple flowers that grew last summer in the vegetable garden. I breathed in as deeply as possible as I hugged her, hoping to capture enough of her aroma to store in my memory. We agreed to get together for tea one day soon; I've had tea with her so many times, as we've discussed the mechanism for absorbing the sun's heat in the sun room, the tiers in the vegetable garden, the blower on the fireplace, the heater and the vents in the greenhouse, the narrow shelves for cans in the basement, and the way each window has its own lovely view of the Sligo valley. Although all these conversations have been imaginary, they seem as real as any that we might actually have one day soon.

This past Monday at the sale barn, in came Frank, asking for his usual coffee in a ceramic, not Styrofoam, cup. "Hey, Chicago," (he calls me that since he found out I lived there), "I have a present for you." It turns out he found a kitten at the sale barn a few days earlier and had taken it home, cared for it, made a bed out of one of his old work shirts, named it Barney because he found him at the barn. He seems like a gruff old man; he never mentions his wife; I met his son when we bought a tiller in town –the son and daughter-in-law own the store and when they talk of Frank you know they understand that he is a character in the community. He said to me, "I can kill a person or an animal, but I can't tolerate the abuse of any creature." Wee Barney now resides in an extra large dog crate just outside the chicken coop in the chicken house. His accommodations include a cat box, a snuggly bed, water and food dishes and kitten toys. He has playtime regularly throughout the day and will grow up with hens as mother figures. Jenny told me Frank will sometimes tell stories about his days out west working on movie sets.

It has taken me this long to appreciate the way the trees flower in springtime like a new poem each day. The robins and bluebirds return, the bees and raccoons and skunks wake up and it seems like the spirits of the living and the dead join the world as it comes to life. There is hardly a silent moment: hundreds of birds sing at once, the wind swishes the leaves and howls now and then, the frogs in the trees fill the night with their chuckling and whining.

There is a deep purple iris growing right in between two tiers in the vegetable garden. So typical of the Viola I know.

Rose, you unfold
into butterfly
up, and away you go

News From Sligo

June 11

Perspective can be a complex phenomenon. A tree, for example, can look like broccoli from an airplane. But when you stand under one, you are small. Lying in a hammock, you look up into the aerial green world and imagine life as a creature in the air, branches and knots and crooks as landmarks.

A few weeks ago, a storm came through that brought the weather radio to life every few minutes, each time the National Weather Service issued a new tornado, thunderstorm or flash flood warning for the area. Ross was in town, twenty miles away at the office; the dogs, silent and serious, accompanied me to the basement. We called each other back and forth as the storms came through. In Salem, the sky grew dark; the rain and the wind roared, beating their way through. The customers and employees across the street at the restaurant joined the real estate office staff in the basement. Trees fell, bringing down power lines. A call came in notifying Wanda that her barn was in pieces, the roof across the road. People quietly used their cell phones in the darkness to check on their children, their wives and husbands and neighbors.

In our Sligo basement, the dogs looked up from dark hiding places as I watched leafy branches, wind and rain like a crazy car wash out a small window. A flash, a vibrating boom, and the lights were out.

By the time I emerged from the basement, the sun was shining and the birds were singing. As I looked out the front door I realized the source of the crash I had heard: a white oak tree, about three feet in diameter and about 75 feet tall lay, a fallen giant, halfway between the house and the road. It missed the power line that crosses our front yard by about three feet. Over the next few weeks I would watch its new bright green leaves turn brown, as the leaves on the other trees grew larger and darker green.

It was Friday, and there would be a sale that evening at the livestock auction barn. Jenny and I expected that with so much damage in and around the town, trees on houses and roads, and no power anywhere, if they decided to have a sale at all, there would probably not be many people there. At about three in the afternoon, I arrived at the diner and found it dark; one of the windows had imploded and been replaced by a large square of plywood. We would be cooking everything on a gas stove; candles lit up the tables with help from a few electric lights run off a generator, which would also keep the refrigerators running. We would serve more people than any previous Friday night. I think they came because they could have hot food, find out who was okay and who needed help; and after exchanging stories about downed fences and blocked roads, the lack of water and the fact that the power might be out for ten days, the new reality would seem less like a dream.

Troy's family has had roots in this part of the Missouri Ozarks for generations. He knows more about trees than I could ever imagine. He knows trees from the perspective of a logger, but also as a scientist. Ross told about our fallen tree at the office, so Beth brought her husband over to the house to plan the removal. Beth is like that. She just solves problems for people. Troy is big and strong and wields a very large chainsaw like a toy. From the ends of the branches in, he cut fireplace-sized logs, and we are now transporting them to the woodshed a wheel barrow full at a time. When they are all out of the way, he will return to take the trunk. Maybe it will be made into two-by-fours and become part of a new home.

Gathering each log from its place on the ground, walking around and in the tree's limbs like a Lilliputian around Gulliver, the perspective is new. It is an amazing structure. The tree branches out and down through its roots, up and out from its trunk through its limbs; and from the core to the bark, one thin circle each year, over decades it becomes a giant that weighs tons. The tree was a city of birds and squirrels, of moles and worms, cicadas in the summer, thousands of humming bees in the spring. In our autopsy we are disassembling it, and for the first time, as I help take it apart, I see how it was able to stand for a hundred years. And as I lift the logs from the place on the ground where a whole limb lay, and move the smaller branches out of the way, the shape of the fallen tree no longer resembles a tree. I think about how I'll split the logs in a few months, how I'll remember from last year that you gradually get a feel for the way the fibers run in the wood and splitting becomes easier. We lived one summer in the shade of this tree towering over us, as did Viola and John some thirty-five summers before we arrived. Before that, it grew for seven or eight decades above other families in a house long gone. It will keep us warm for a couple of winters to come. Thank you, tree.

September 9

Just across the road, in the middle of a field, there is an old abandoned house from a hundred years ago when Sligo was a thriving town of four thousand inhabitants. It has silently become visible, like a ghost, through the thick mist each morning for the past few weeks, as dawn approaches and the dogs and I walk down the road and back. A big oak tree stands on each side and the scene is of a cold bygone coziness. I can imagine a small family, moments before anyone awakes. The fire will appear orange behind the windows; smoke will rise from the chimney. Soon, off the father will go, down the road to the furnace, the children to the schoolhouse. Then Osito races ahead in pursuit of a rabbit, and I take another sip of coffee and squint into a foggy field in search of the outlines of the horses. I won't allow myself to think about the school day until we've gone back inside.

This summer was not like last summer. It was just as full of surprises and treasures, but each year grows in its own way. I battled weeds every week in the garden, but it was much more under control than last year. I made my way down to each and every tier, and something was planted on each level. First-time crops included potatoes, sweet potatoes, okra, mustard greens, collard greens, broccoli, cauliflower, cabbage, bok choy, turnips, and beets. I had no tomato worms this year, but the squash bugs did me in worse than ever: two zucchini, two pumpkins, three summer squash, and then it was all gone. And they attempted to devour the watermelons, but apparently didn't like them. I followed my friend Sarah's example from last summer and planted lots of zinnias, marigolds, and nasturtiums. I enjoy walking around, inspecting everything, and eating the nasturtiums right there. I doubt that we will enjoy much of the broccoli, cabbage and greens. The rabbits are snacking there regularly and the electric poultry fence is over around the orchard.

I had to send the chickens over there to control the Japanese beetle population. There were no Japanese beetles last summer. And the squirrels did not eat my apples and pears and peaches last year. I had so much fruit I didn't know what to do with it all. This summer, the only one who was able to enjoy a peach or two was Poptart, who plucked a couple off a branch that was hanging over the fence. I found dozens of peach pits on the ground. It seems the squirrels and chickens teamed up, the ones picking and tasting a peach, then tossing it down to the others, who pecked it clean. I purchased three fourths of a bushel of peaches at the market so I could make some jam. If I'm lucky I might get some of John's famous Arkansas black apples in November. Right now there are plenty on the tree. And there are still a few green pears.

The blackberries came and went: there were not many, they dried up fast, and they were not very juicy. Ross and I spent a few hours one Sunday walking all over sixty or so acres and brought back less than a gallon. And the plums, what plums?

One evening I arrived home from a road trip and Ross showed me where Osito was attacked and had four holes in his side, scaring me to tears. But he survived. And there were so few ticks this summer. And the creek was cool and full of the best swimming holes ever. And I bought eight more pullets from Melvin and they have begun to lay such an assortment of eggs. And I finally met Viola in town for lunch and she told me wonderful stories. And I made dozens of new friends at the sale barn. Frank entrusted Wee Barney to my care, and Janis and Don sent us Cooper to keep him company. Now the two of them run the chicken house and keep all rodents away from the house and outbuildings (a mouse nest almost destroyed our riding mower, causing Ross much anguish; though I was so proud of him as he took it all in stride and kept the lawn looking like a golf course with only a reel mower and a push mower during the interminable weeks the riding mower was in the shop).

During the last weeks of my employment at the sale barn diner, I helped Jenny clean the entire place (sale block, offices and seating area included), because Annette's husband broke both legs in a motorcycle crash and she had to take care of him instead of doing the cleaning. One Wednesday afternoon I arrived to find a strange white creature lying on the ground in a pen in the back. It was after a Tuesday night sale, where any and all creatures are brought to auction. After a few minutes, I realized it was a rabbit whose head was twisted around, ears towards the ground. Larry the barn guy said he was going to release it in a nearby field unless I wanted to take it home. He was supposed to kill it, but he just couldn't bring himself to do it. And Larry is not a squeamish man; the week before, I kept hearing a bang followed by squealing, and later learned from him that he had been "martyring hogs". The sale barn is not, by a long shot, a place for the weak of stomach. Of course, I brought the rabbit home, named it Silly Wabbit, and proceeded to research his condition on the Internet. It seems he has *torticollis*, or "head tilt", which could be caused by an ear infection, ear mites, or something else. A round of antibiotics has not cured him. My next plan is ear mite treatment. He has no trouble eating and drinking, but he does look pitiful.

Ross is relieved that I will not be back to the sale barn for a long, long time. His patience has been stretched to its limit as our zero population growth policy has been trampled to shreds.

Yes, it has been a beautiful, rewarding summer, complete with hummingbirds, skies full of stars, breathtaking horseback rides, guaranteed fishing and lovely fish fries, creek swims and sheer joy.

And I will remember each moment fondly while I am teaching Spanish at Salem High School this year. I consider myself fortunate to have happened upon this opportunity at this point in my life. I am learning where college students come from. Adolescents, as I now recall once again after so many long years of not being one, have much in common with eighteen-month old dogs: they are naturally distracted by any new idea that pops into their heads or movement within their range of perception; they have minute attention spans and must be constantly occupied to prevent them from becoming destructive; and their hormones cause them to suffer chronic emotional upheaval. They are also irresistibly fun and funny and bright, and conveniently forgetful of the most recent unpleasantness they might have experienced with their trainer or teacher.

I have attended not only my first ever high school football game, but also the first one to take place in a town the size of Salem, where everyone attends

118

the game and is as much a faithful fan as city people are of professional teams; maybe more. I learned that the only times the Walmart is empty are when there are football games at the high school.

I am beginning to see that during one year in the country I learned to live by a different clock and a different calendar. Squeezing myself into this new routine is like trying on a pair of saddle shoes from eighth grade. Wearing them is not so difficult as long as I can wake up and go to bed in my comfy old house shoes.

News From Sligo

Drop by drop
water solidifies into
crooked fingers of glass

February 9

The quiet life has had some changes over the past months, though it is generally still quiet here in Sligo. I recall a book by Joel Salatin by the title *You Can Farm*. I read it several years ago, and it encouraged me to believe that our dream of living in the country could actually happen, providing me with countless themes for daydreaming. One piece of advice that comes to mind frequently is that if you have a job away from your farm you will never be able to live off of your farm work. It has taken me over a year to understand that the life we have now and the life Mr. Salatin proposes are not the same; I concede that I am not a purist, and I accept this.

All of this to say that Ross and I spend almost all of our time not working here at home, but rather doing many of the same things we did before: I teach; he teaches, counsels, and works one day a week in the flat-lining real estate business. At the end of the day (literally), though, we enjoy the privilege of each aspect of our life here, all the more precious because we are working hard to keep it.

Each day is as full of discovery as it was a year ago. Although I cannot say that teaching in a public high school is anything approximating a dream come true, I certainly never dreamed I would one day find myself doing just that. After the initial months of adjustment, which were in many ways terrible, I am happy to report that no one has sustained permanent injury and I now enjoy going to work. I am amazed several times each day. There is nothing tedious or boring, and it is definitely entertaining.

I have come to understand, however, that the consequences of not taking this job seriously are disastrous on every scale. How is it that once we are no longer teenagers, the teenager as such becomes inscrutable? I have learned that we must negotiate a common ground, and although they do not appear to take anything seriously, they do; the adult who does not appreciate this will pay dearly. The adult lives in a rational world of order, a tree establishing roots and focusing on one kind of growth at a time; the teenager lives in a continuous flow of sensation, a butterfly taking from one flower then the next, indiscriminate and reactive.

I guess it is irrelevant at this point to ask ourselves how we came to believe, as a society, that we should confine them for seven or eight hours daily to chairs in rooms where they are supposed to practice sustained intellectual attention; or why we have removed fitness as a real objective from Physical Education, depriving them of the opportunity to release some of the energy built up through the volatile combination of presumably edible processed chemicals ingested via the federal surplus food disposal program at lunch, and hormones on the roller coaster ride of adolescence.

So one must accept that the individual high school-aged student, whose natural tendency is toward hypersensitivity, melodrama, chaos, rebellion, elation and hyper-stimulation, will develop an *attitude* in an environment that does not provide captivating and diversified opportunities to direct all that explosive creativity into something productive. Again, the consequences of not taking this seriously are disastrous. There is a foolish authoritarian desire to repress; but really, that makes about as much sense as a second mortgage to pay off a huge credit card debt: it just postpones the day when it will all blow up in our faces.

I suspect that teaching in a rural school has

allowed me a perspective that would be impossible in a city school, where the effects of the structure are too overwhelming. And entering the system as a college professor with a profusion of unfounded opinions and no real understanding has provided me with a view independent of anyone else in this small community of administrators and educators. My greatest advantage, though, has definitely been that I've mostly had to rely on my students to teach me what this is really all about. I am with them all the time. Up to my neck. I've always promoted immersion as the best way to learn to communicate in a foreign language. Survival is a strong motivator. And they have forced me not only to make every effort to understand them, but also to search for the answer to the question we all share: what is the purpose of public education?

Blame my conservative neighbors, the small-town obsession with patriotism, some incipient ingenuousness, but I have come to believe that public education is not essentially preparation for college. Its primary purpose is to develop citizens and prepare them for democracy. Like a free press, it is a foundational component. The one ensures diverse and limitless sources of information; and the other, the ability to interpret and assimilate ideas, ponder them with a critical mind, and produce independent, well-founded thoughts and opinions --and the ability to discriminate among issues, opinions, information and propaganda. At this level as well, the consequences of not taking public education seriously are disastrous.

So I have uncovered a new aspect of this life in the country –a purpose that furthers and consolidates the experiment of living in a different way. I was looking for a simple, direct way to understand life by understanding what we eat. I've begun to practice eating conscientiously. Looking into the sustenance of life has led me to explore its purposes in a simple, direct way as well. It is a little bit poetic that when I have sought distance I have felt closer to discovering the occasional truth. As I observe that the way in which the government feeds our children reflects the way in which the government teaches them, I am a little saddened to acknowledge that in theory we are the government.

Thanksgiving in the Hills, a Sligo Tale

Around here hunting is an endeavor in which the entire community appears to unite for a season in common heritage. A thin line of SUVs hauling ATV-laden trailers brings in folks from urban centers two or three hours away to partake in the reenactment of an ancient ritual of survival. There are even days established especially for children to hone and display their skills.

Almost everyone pursues deer, but occasionally there stands the individual who is after a wild turkey, perhaps imagining that first Thanksgiving and a table that would bring together the splendid bounty that nature offered first to the Native Americans in exchange for a season's worth of labor and a prayer.

I choose to believe that these were the primary impressions tickling Ross's imagination when he decided that the moment had come for him to join in the ancient tradition of trekking out into the woods, waiting, watching, aiming, shooting, and finally transporting home the dead, field-dressed beast from the wild to feed his family.

Anyone who is even marginally acquainted with Ross knows that any new project he undertakes is carried out slowly and with exhaustive research, practice, and forethought. Over the years he has acquired an impressive collection of apparel suitable for hunting, in both orange and camouflage. He has been a long distance runner almost since birth, and has an enviable set of muscles. His dexterity and coordination compare well with those of the native inhabitants of the continent who first slay deer, wild turkey, squirrel, and the occasional mountain lion. All of this, along with his tenaciously earned classification of Eagle Scout, seems to have led to this precise turn in his life's path. A few days spent with a bow and arrow, sharpening his sight, reminding his fingers, chest and biceps; he was ready to set out for the centerpiece of our Thanksgiving dinner.

The fact that it was his birthday contributed an almost poetic aura to the occasion. He carried the tree stand on one shoulder, the bow and arrow on the other, and a small backpack with a few supplies. He easily hiked the three miles to his selected spot in the woods. Tree stand assembled, weaponry in place, he climbed to his nest and silently watched the world come to life around him. He must have asked himself at least once during these hours, as he went over in his mind each step leading to the final moment, whether he would really be able to carry this project through to its deadly end. In many ways it seems contrary to all he stands for philosophically. This endeavor, in fact, symbolically divides his self into two: the hunter and the philosopher, the man of the mind and the man of nature.

It is not for me to know the content of his silent conversation with his conscience as he watched and waited. All I can say is that there was a smile among the few streaks of blood on his dirty face when he stood on the threshold, a larger-than-life silhouette filling the door frame: in his outstretched, brawny, calloused hands, what first caught my eye were the silent shiny black eyes of the most lovely and delectable wild *Tofurkey* upon which either of us has ever dined.

Little armadillo hands
wove this path.
I'm just following.

www.ingramcontent.com/pod-product-compliance
Lightning Source LLC
Chambersburg PA
CBHW030021290326
41934CB00005B/431